Suburban Sutras

poems by

Austin Sanchez-Moran

Finishing Line Press
Georgetown, Kentucky

Suburban Sutras

Copyright © 2021 by Austin Sanchez-Moran
ISBN 978-1-64662-639-7 First Edition
All rights reserved under International and Pan-American Copyright Conventions.
No part of this book may be reproduced in any manner whatsoever without written
permission from the publisher, except in the case of brief quotations embodied in
critical articles and reviews.

ACKNOWLEDGMENTS

"The Spleen of Affluence" first appeared in *Midwestern Gothic* and was
    entitled, "The Spleen of Affluenza"
"Monologue to the Moon" first appeared in *Fjords Review*
"Dream of a Disappearing Actor", "The Founder's Day Race and the
    Pink Cakes", and "Barber Shop in a Chinese Restaurant" all first
    appeared in *Yalobusha Review*
"Instructional Poem #1" first appeared in *Salamander Magazine*
"Instructional Poem #2" first appeared in *Rivet Journal*
"Listening to Lolita, Driving West Through Oklahoma" first appeared in
    Yemassee Journal
"Bank Vault Dinner Party" and "Day in the Manner of Magritte" first
    appeared in *Maudlin House*
"Being Caught in a Failing State" first appeared in *RHINO 2018* Poetry and
    was chosen for *Best MicroFiction* 2020
"Heat Dream of Illinois" was chosen for the anthology, *Best New Poets of the
    Midwest*
"The Courtyard Orange Tree at Soledad" first appeared in *The Soledad
    Inmates' Journal*
"Ballad of Black Stuntman" first appeared in *Linden Avenue Literary Journal*

Publisher: Leah Huete de Maines
Editor: Christen Kincaid
Cover Art: Louis Boutan, Wikimedia Commons, Public Domain
Author Photo: Beverly Sanchez
Cover Design: Elizabeth Maines McCleavy

Order online: www.finishinglinepress.com
            also available on amazon.com

Author inquiries and mail orders:
Finishing Line Press
P. O. Box 1626
Georgetown, Kentucky 40324
U. S. A.

Table of Contents

"Nothing cheers him, darts, tennis, falconry,
his people dying by the balcony"
—Baudelaire, "Spleen" (Trans. by Robert Lowell)

"The dream is always the same."
—Joel Goodson, from *Risky Business*

The Spleen of Affluence

"I've been awake all night. It's terrible."
—Charles Schweppe's Suicide Note

Prologue

John Hughes sips coffee, reads the Tribune
and mumbles something angsty and sublime
in his bathrobe, in his driveway, exhausted
with his own teenagers, as we pass by him in our yellow
bus, that takes us past the leafy, silhouetting sidewalks
towards a school near the cemetery and a deep ravine.

I.

He greeted me in a Tartan smoking jacket,
then showed me his single-edged hunting knife.
It had a Stag handle with a Damascus steel blade.
His dad had helped my dad get a client, so I had
to play with him while my dad toured the mansion.
Soon before my dad left, I was convinced to stay.

I slept scared in a bed that had posts and drapery.
I awoke to a Samurai sword shining in my face.
He then took me to a sunny conservatory with a Grand
Piano, poured orange juice from a glass decanter
and turned on "Dune". It was the first time I had fallen
asleep and woken up two different times during a movie.

II.

What happened to me when I lost the ferret
after it bit me and ran off in the State Treasurer's basement?
Was I spanked or just not invited back?
And what happened to me when I was caught teaching
one of my female classmates, "Doctor" in her bedroom?
Was I hit and dragged away or were my parents called?

1

My best friend, Will and I had backyards that backed up
to one another. At our bus stop we teased a girl
with glasses. We made fun of the minister's son.
We beat up the kid who wore an earring in his right ear.
We threw snowballs from afar at the bigger kids
and even broke some of our neighbor's windows.

III.

The Walgreen family adopted three Russian girls.
One of them was in my class and one day she called my house
and because I didn't know how to answer the phone yet,
a message was left, "Hi. This is Olga, calling for Austin.
Hi, Austin. You're funny. I like your brown hair.
And, and, and, I love you."

Sam was the kid who only ate Cocoa Puffs and pasta.
He invited a bunch of us to watch "R" rated movies
on his big screen. And by three, everyone had fallen
asleep and when I went to the kitchen to get a drink,
I saw Sam's mom outside by the edge of the pool, naked.
But did she see me, as she dove into the lit, green waters?

IV.

On Christmas Eve, my family would walk across the street
to a party where all the children had to sing or dance or
perform a skit. Once though, Santa showed up
with weird breath and sat me on his knee and asked me
what I wanted,—"A hockey stick." "Oh, I hope you don't
want two because then you'll go to H-E-double hockey sticks."

Later that winter, I noticed the eyes of the man
who sharpened my skates and zambonied the ice.
During the games we played on the outdoor rink,
parents would line the boards cheering at their children,
and my sister would bring over whiskey
in a thermos to my dad as it flurried.

V.
The heir to a pair of historic Chicago hotels told me
he wanted me to come over and play some new video games.
As his au pair dropped us off in the pebbled driveway,
his dad's green Jaguar roadster came rumbling behind us.
The car drove into its own garage, continuing to run.
We waited for a few moments, then went inside.

I was brought up to a loft in the vast fifth floor attic.
I looked out over the thick forest to the shimmering lake.
We played the video games on piles of stuffed animals
while he ordered us snacks through an intercom.
To me, he joked, "I didn't want to have to play this all alone."
It grew dark and his father never came in from the garage.

VI.

After I was called "Taco" again on the bus ride home,
I crawled up the green-carpeted stairs with the iron
handrails, to the pink attic closet filled with square, red
vinyl suitcases and thick down coats. I would stay there
until my mother came home and cooked us dinner.
My stucco house had green awnings that shaded my room.

Other days, after getting dropped off from a sports practice,
I would open the door to arguments, my sister was eating
or not eating enough, or someone had to do more work
around the house, but many times the discussion would calm
and move toward the prospect of travel. How large
the world could seem when everything was in its place.

Epilogue

When we got to school we were immediately sent home.
One of my classmates died when a car seat fell on her.
She had suffocated. My mom said I needed to be careful
at all times now. That night, I dreamt I lay in the way
back of my station wagon with the groceries and watched
the seat come down and I did nothing to help her.

Heat Dream of Illinois

Just as words are just
the husk of meaning,
we have been seeking
the checkering meat
of gold embering
and white stalking sun.

But then it must be
always the autumn
at best, Illini
summers chilled with bite,
tightening each cob,
still enclosed in green.

So we must each find
this tasseled, toughest
sister, who can share
her soiled, silking
secret for silence,
"There is no need for words."

Instructional Poem #1

After Yoko Ono

Tulips and chimneys
and ash and dirt and
honey and salt and
hives and the ocean

and hide until everyone goes
home, until everyone forgets
about you, hide everything
until everyone dies

in hives under the ocean

salt the honey,
                ash the dirt
and tulips will grow
                out of the chimneys

After "Riot"

After the poem by Gwendolyn Brooks

"Riot is the language of the unheard."
                              —Martin Luther King

*"The Dream thrives on generalization, on limiting the number of
possible questions, on privileging immediate answers."*
                              —Ta-Nehisi Coates

I.

We would rush home from the bus stop
and sit on high stools eating Fluff
and peanut butter sandwiches with the crusts
cut off. "The brown part is burnt," my friend
explained to me, "Why would you eat that?"
and his mother always appeased her clever son.

Then we would watch RealTV
to see if we'd see someone die.
The gasoline tanker exploded,
took out an entire city block, but the driver survived.
And the Coast Guard helicopter gathered up
the black man in the rescue basket, wet and scared.
And they brought him safely to dry land.
Was there no one else inside the flooded house?

"No one really dies on TV," my friend said to me,
"They're not allowed to show all that."
I would get picked up later by my mother,
and every night I'd sleep soundly.

II.

Where I grew up black people mostly lived on TV.
Michael Jordan with tongue-out concentration,
a sweet black body, soaring above the rim.
Sammy Sosa trotting, after another ball flew into
the stands, and then he blew kisses at the camera.

Some weekends I'd be taken down to the South Side,
under the Skyway, to a homeless shelter, where once
a gaunt man screamed at me for more fish sticks.
And another time an old woman with a mustache
told me that her food was crap, everything was crap.

But no poem is made of just words of the silenced
or the actions of my heroes. No understanding
came from leaving language untranslated, tuned out.
Parents say, "shut up, the children will hear." But I grow still,
listening to the frequency of the language of the unheard.

III.   *For Dr. Chala Holland*

To disembark   they must   dig out

                    EXIT

To leave   their   comfort zones

To try to   dream   from the other side

They are white and well mannered.
They are pretty and they never sweat.
They are clean and they are everywhere.

Have they given a second thought to consciousness?
Have they given a second thought to consciousness?

Why do   these people   offend
                              themselves?

            Do I dare?

                    It's time   it's time

                    to help   these people.

Listening to Lolita, Driving West Through Oklahoma

I guess I shouldn't start with all of those unattended oil rigs
        penetrating the dry earth like clockwork.

Those lines of wind turbines creating a pinwheel effect
        are in fact the new nymphets of the west.

And isn't the average American male supposed to fall in love
        with whatever destiny manifests?

Updike said, "This is the truest love story of the 20th century,"
        but Updike's dead and it's the 21st.

I look to my left, a black bovine mass of thousands huddle
        around the circular water troughs.

A couple are copulating as they struggle for space, sinking
        into their manure, waiting for slaughter.

I look to my right, the neon Texan is pointing at a 72 oz. steak.
        Always an hour out of somewhere.

There is dust collecting in the corners of my windshield
        and two questions are getting mixed up

in my head, "Am I on the run?" and "What have I done
        to deserve this grotesque awe, America?"

After *Freaks*

Directed by Todd Browning (1932)

Cleopatra, Queen of the Flying Trapeze,
They accepted you, offered up a loving cup—

The Stork Woman danced her white tablecloth
champagne dance, a peacock feather in her fancy hat.

And the leopard-printed third-gendered Tarzan
joined in, "We accept her, we accept her, one of us!"

Then the Italian dwarf passed around the oversized coupe,
and all the pinheaded twins giggled and drank along.

And the Bearded Lady began, "Gooble, gobble, gooble gobble,"
and The Half Boy, conducted them all with a butter knife.

But you laughed in their faces, tossed wine on their party
and told them they were filthy, slimy freaks. Unable

to see their sideshow struggle for a happy life.
So why were you so horrifyingly surprised when

they all came after you? It was your venomous asp
angry and dispatched, crawling in the mud of a thunderstorm,

and the last thing you saw after your wagon crashed,
and you woke up chicken, scared and squawking, tarred and feathered,

was The Human Snake, a limbless black man with a knife
between his teeth, who came to cut off your legs.

Day in the Manner of Magritte

There is a man in a charcoal wool suit who parks his black Mini in a tall concrete car park in the middle of a sheep farm in Devon, England. He walks out into a field of tall grass to a mowed opening where there is a long, thin, crudely made, wooden table. He sits down on a stool and places his bowler next to an empty white plate. Soon after, he is served green apple slices smothered in clotted cream. He eats and continues until he begins to feel sick. As he is slowing down, a cannon is placed in front of him on the other side of the table, aimed at his head. He then throws up into a metal bucket at his side that has been provided for him. He continues eating and vomiting for the entire day. At dusk, as he walks back to the car park, he looks out across the rolling hills, all squarely divided by crumbling stone fences, and on top of one distant green hill there is a skipping record on a golden gramophone that is repeating, "Ce n'est pas un emploi?" (Translation: Is this not a job?)

Legend of the Happy Swimming Pool

A Found Poem

I.
Do you know the most heartbreaking of all dreams?
I'll tell you what mine is.
And I've dreamed it maybe three times in my life
And I hope I die dreaming it.
…

I call it the Legend of the Happy Swimming Pool—
I'm somewhere in the neighborhood, where I grew up…
And I go down a street that I've never been on before
there was no reason ever to go there
and there is a marvelous swimming pool,
marvelous girls, who are crazy about me
and there's this sense of "Where have you been?,
We've been waiting for you, all these years…"
…

II.
You know this feeling though,
that there is something in your life,
that all you have to do is turn a corner
or open a door and it'll all be so…

I don't fear the nightmare,
I can take any nightmare.
I fear the dream, which is good,
which has the reality,
that we can't achieve in reality.
I don't fear the nightmare,
I fear those tears
of loss and deprivation.

When you are at the happy swimming pool
which is kind of like Eden, you see
for a few minutes
of one anonymous suburban night
and is forever gone,
I fear the end of a happy dream.

The Founder's Day Race and The Pink Cakes

Each August an Illinois town celebrates its incorporation with a week long carnival in the large, grassy central square. There are popcorn and cotton candy makers, amusement park rides, clowns, ponies. And it all culminates in, "The Founder's Day Race", where the county mausoleum opens up the crypts of the two founders of the town, dead now for over a century, and positions the bodies into modified mannequin stands that hold their legs, waists and necks in place, as they are shipped to the back of the beloved local bakery in a decorated hearse. Meanwhile, two eight-foot tall cakes, with an inner-mold that keeps the center of the cake hollow, are baked. Each cake is then lifted up with a forklift and carefully placed on top of each founder, encasing them. Finally, the fragile cakes are walked down the street on dollies to the square.

The captain of the football team and the mayor traditionally run the race. It is a 200-yard straight sprint. At 50 yards the cakes are placed side by side and both runners dash up to the cake and hug it until they uncover each founder. With pink frosting and yellow cake all over their bodies, they carry their founder by the belt and neck as arms flail. After another 50 yards, there are 2 canvases on easels. Each runner dips the founder's finger or hand into a blue inkwell and creates an abstract painting. After each runner is satisfied with their work, which can take up to a half hour, they drop their body and sprint to the finish line. They are met with wild applause as they are hosed off. Behind them a swarm of children run onto the race path, stuffing their mouths with the pieces of cake, off of the dollies, the grass, and off of the founder's bodies.

Lake Forest Chainsaw Massacre

A South Side project kid moves on up,
the new owner of an Armour Estate.

> *"Violating an unwritten code*
> *of aesthetics."*

Then, one grey spring day, laying in bed,
cow-licked Mandinka haircut, gold-chained
                        chest at rest,

> **"...to see how my ancestors,**
> **who were slaves, felt."**

the African Warrior with allergies,
decides to cut down some Oak trees
                        on his property.

> *"That precious commodity..."*

The concerned citizens of this genteel suburb
take up arms for their beloved enclosing
                        of green canopy.

> *"If he doesn't like trees*
> *why didn't he build a house*
> *in the cornfields?"*

But even when the neighborhood boys came
to ask, he signed all of their paper autographs.

> *"An act of sheer butchery."*

So with pollen in his sinuses, wood chips flying
onto his gold chains and bracelets, he just smirks,

> **"I pity the fool[s]."**

How Fruit Got Their Colors

After Frida Kahlo

I scuffled on all fours through a dirt field,
kicking up the dead vines, hungry for toad skin.

Canaries flew overhead, spreading yellow
over another patch of white melons baking in sun.

An old woman recited ailments from her arthritis
in Spanish, wearing a dark hood to cover her antlers.

I bathed under an almond tree that hung tiny sundials,
blushing with a toad skin grin as the flowers blushed back.

Her voice, then, upwardly inflecting, repeated a question.
I told myself, "Just say, 'Sí.'" and I said it. She did not agree.

She threw a prickly pear at me, "Que feo reptil!"
I palmed it and dined in the dirt, my blood dyeing the bulb.

Brandenburg Concerto No. 5 in G Major

I'm in an orchestra pit that is flooding
from beneath as everyone is tuning up.
It's an insouciant droning and fiddling,

a piece of music they'll never play again,
a picture being painted outside of the frame,
a picture being painted before anything.

All the practiced stage actors hate it,
thinking the strings are taut enough,
that the reeds have been moistened.

They just can't tell where it's coming from,
as the water spews from the broken pipes
up past our knees, and I start to dance.

Being Caught in a Failing State

I wake up in a Holiday Inn in a Former Soviet Bloc nation. I walk down the stairs to the lobby where there are men with guns saying they are members of the "Green Revolution". One knocks me out with the butt of his rifle.

I wake up in a cell that looks like the small chamber room of a medieval castle. I am still wearing pajamas. There are a couple other men that have just woken up dirty and confused. Before any conversation, a soldier opens the door and throws gardening equipment at us. "Work! Go!" We walk out and down a long, dark hallway to fields where others in pajamas are harvesting plants and others are hoeing the parched ground. Another soldier points and says, "That is tomato basil leaf crossbred and that is cactus aloe crossbred. You two over there, you, over here. Work."

I wake up the next morning and the cell's wall has crumbled and we all walk out of the hole where the window had been. We run towards the small city in the distance arriving to a crowd watching a large military parade and on one side of the main square a barricaded corner has a banner labeled, "Tourists". I run through the crowds sneaking up to two Brits in safari garb taking photographs. I open my mouth to ask, "Is this a coup?" but a lemon rind is suctioned to my teeth. The male tourist says, "I think this one needs help." And then the woman counters, "He's dirty though..." I'm screaming to say anything now. "Not a talkative fellow I see... Let's leave him." Tanks enter the square.

Monologue to the Moon

"Poems are bullshit unless they are/teeth or trees or lemons piled/on a step."
—Amiri Baraka

Tonight, I can only answer you in large portions.
Do we still need a sitcom laugh track in a world of missing persons?

They said it was a good time for lilac, for plumbing, for urban plight.
This is how I'll separate day from night.

I noticed a dead wasp in the sun on the windowsill.
Just the urge to drink the morning's mercury makes me ill.

My Buick puked again in reticent Connecticut, sitting sappy under a tree.
Engine endorphins, a well-oiled, steely gland fantasy.

How come the tides don't bother me?
Are we sure you are the goddess we want?

I can be a tightly packed revolutionary!
I can squeeze lemon into the sea urchin's orifice,
                as he struggles to draw with a gull's tail feather!

My mother was a manta ray, shelf life electric!
My father could play the blues if he was a tuna fish sandwich!

Attorneys are sleepily marching back from you, milk jug in hand.
And gold-toothed, sweater-vested investors are only drinking
                the wine that has hints of a wet dog's neck.

This report is brought to you from a lion's claw-foot bathtub
                in shining sand, wet with your perspiration.

The Blue Backhoe

Cars park along the street of a yet to be finished development of mid-sized McMansions on the edge of the prairie. Formally dressed young couples walk up to the red door of one newly completed powder blue Cape Cod with white trim. As each new couple knocks the golden pineapple door knocker, the couple that lives in the house opens the door, looks surprised and grateful, and welcomes them in out of the cool evening.

Next door there is a wooden box frame of an unfinished house with plastic coverings flapping in the wind and tools left on the ground. On top of the frame there is a cast iron skillet in place of a roof. In the skillet lie two 10-foot long, 3-foot thick sticks of butter. And, in between the two houses, there is a rusty, blue backhoe.

The party blasts Bossa Nova as everyone yells and laughs over it, getting increasingly louder. Then, after an hour, the blue backhoe suddenly swivels, scoops up a stick of butter and swings its dipper back toward the completed home. The stick flies through the tall kitchen window, striking and killing the two owners who were busily preparing more hors d'oeuvres. It then scoops up the other stick and swings towards the living room. This time the butter breaks the window jambs and takes out the granite chimney, smashing the fireplace, damaging the entire right side of the house, crushing and burning its' guests. A grandfather clock falls on one man. A chandelier drops onto another woman. There are eight dead in total.

The next morning, builders come back to their house and see the damage next door, wondering how it all could have happened. As they walk through the red front door, bodies float toward them in butter.

Taking Advantage

After Michael Robbins

I have a dream…
I'll one day run a Ponzi scheme.
I cried when I wrote this song,
so sue me if I play it strong.

I made this mistake of Burberrian proportions.
The plaid bride stripped bare by her contortions.
Is a dream a lie if it don't come true,
or is it something lewd?

To steal my father's whiskey would be
like nothing else in Tennessee.
Bottle of red, bottle of white,
tell me more, tell me more, did she put up a fight?

I'm risking oversaturation
but I belong to the blank generation.
She moves in mysterious ways…
I measure time by how a body sways.

Tenth Avenue Freeze-Out.
Ten devils in the freezer.
My ice-cubed friends are Doug and Skeeter.
I got a bad case of the gout.

It was all a big buyout bid,
you ain't never been a virgin, kid,
you were fucked from the start,
in the foul rag and bone shop of the heart.

The Courtyard Orange Tree at Soledad Prison

For all of the lifers

Reminds me of the great white
marble fountains of Venice,
sculpted next to the flooding
canals in the spring.

We must always remember
we're mostly made of water.

Prisoners in the long hall!
Remember, we are mostly
made of water, left
to quench our own thirsts.

Legacy

My grandfather left
my grandmother when
my father was one.

They were divorced by two.

My dad, the not-quite-bastard.

The gifts of inheritance,
are harsh and artless.

The Chickadee

I spilled blue oil-based paint in the basement
trying to finish my pinewood derby car on my own.
I stained my palms and my father yelled
and grabbed my left wrist hard, (I had recently broken it)
and he rubbed a turpentine rag into my hands.

The next day we were driving to a Cubs game
and at the end of a block we saw two Blue Jays
pecking a Chickadee. The little bird was crouched over,
there was already a little blood on the sidewalk,
and my father stopped the car, said, "Go chase
those Blue Jays away, save that bird."
And I ran towards the jays, who flew away,
and the Chickadee couldn't fly, but
it hissed at me, as it hopped away into the brush,
dragging it's left wing on the sidewalk.

We went on to the game and had a great time.
Forgetting about the paint still on my hands.
Forgetting about the injured chickadee.
Forgetting about what happens after
you are saved from wounding.

Dream of a Disappearing Actor

I ring the buzzer to Michael Keaton's apartment in a still un-gentrified part of Brooklyn. We walk, unnoticed, as he tells me he knows a great place to eat lunch. We arrive at a Syrian restaurant and bakery and there is a long line to order. I say I'll stand in line and he says he'll find a table. I notice one of the Zagat reviews hanging in the window claiming the restaurant to be "Backyard Chic" and "a place to get fresh baked pita, and sit at a picnic table with throw away tablecloths." When it is my turn, I order what I had heard the last person in line order, not knowing what to expect. I get my number and then wander down a hall that I think may go towards the restrooms or another seating area. Then, as I get to the end of the narrow hallway, there is a man who moves from my left, out of a walk-in refrigerator, into another room, holding a long machete-like knife. To my right there is a padded cell with old brown bloodstains on the walls. I look further in to see a large, muddy pig hanging upside down from its legs, blindfolded and struggling, but silent. Another man is smiling as he tries to hold its body still. The man with the knife dances around feigning jabs at the pig while he laughs, but also is silent. Before they notice me, I turn and walk back to the restaurant and find it completely empty and Michael Keaton has disappeared.

Bank Vault Dinner Party

I walk into an underground bank vault where my parents have planned a dinner party. There is a long oak table with 3 chairs on both of the long sides of the table. On the table there are 5 mannequin heads and in front of the heads is a pile of wigs. There is only one couple who is seated staring at the faces, figuring out which wig would go best on each head. My mother then comes into the room, stirring a martini, "You should get a baby, renovate that baby, then sell that baby. Flip that baby. I'd be happy with that." She sits down in the third chair, in front of the heads, as I leave the room. I go around the corner to a wall of security deposit boxes. I pull one out and it hits me in the chest, and the top flips open, revealing that it is filled with crushed tomatoes. I grab as much as I can in two cupped hands, carry it back to the main room, and slam down the sloppy mush onto the table.

Fast Food, Love, and Understanding

After a Saturday morning soccer practice
my dad brought me to Burger King
as a special reward for working hard.
As we waited in a line that snaked around the booths,
I could see a crew cut man from the neck up,
unwrapping his meal excitedly.
Then the line began to move ahead faster.
I was asked what I wanted, as the lighted menu
was now legible. I looked up as we shuffled forward,
"A Spicy Chicken Sandwich with no mayo, please."
My dad chuckled. I glanced back at the smiling man.
He was shoving a Whopper into his mouth,
and his blue collared shirt sleeves were rolled up
and his left forearm and hand were a 2-pronged prosthetic.
I stared as the man devoured the rest of it,
licking the ketchup off his shining hooked hand.
Did no one else notice? Was he a kind of superhero?
How did he lose it? My dad took my hand
and brought me to a booth on the other side.
Then, I devoured my sandwich, smiling, holding it
without using my thumb, my 2 fingers each as prongs.

Instructional Poem #2

After Yoko Ono

1. Put a snowflake in a shoebox.

2. Write on the inside, bottom, "You've failed."

3. Close the lid.

4. Write on the top of the lid, "Open it."

5. Give it to your father in winter.

A Composition

Somewhere, someone
is running through dark
forest, holding up the sheet
music that was inspired by you.

That sweaty composer had seen you
sitting in your car, then, indecisively
settling on a slightly bruised tomato
in the mist of the produce aisle.

The composer saw you when you
jogged, slept, talked yourself into being
awake again, and when you grimaced
at the tinny tap water you drank.

The composer looked at you,
and wrote the first note.

Ballad of Black Stuntman

There are times when things get too dangerous.
The scene must be manipulated so as to look real.
But appearances cannot be compromised. Enter Black Stuntman.

Black Stuntman is not automated and can be harmed.
Black Stuntman will crash a car, get bitten by a dog, shot
out of a cannon, then a crew will rush in to extinguish his fear.

He will die in place of you.
He has died for your entertainment.
It will happen again.

It is as if his black body has been snatched,
and put out on the street in place of all of us,
as we watch on a screen, home safe, in our pods.

Then as the pretend policeman approaches,
we still ask, "How does this one end, again?"

Barber Shop in a Chinese Restaurant

I am having dinner with my parents at a Chinese restaurant. It is quiet, with white tablecloths and dim lighting. Only one other couple is eating and whispering to one another in the other corner, as traditional chiming music plays. When we are done with our noodles, waiting for the check, my mother asks me, "Do you want a haircut for dessert?" I walk over to a large barber's chair where a middle-aged Polish woman with long bleach blonde bangs and long pink nails chews gum and says, "Name's 'Trixie', pick a fortune." I lift the cover of the blue Barbicide and then pull on a thin ticker tape that rises out of the disinfectant. The fortune is in Polish. I give the paper to her and she reads it to herself, throws it on the ground, and begins to cut my hair frantically. Then, I notice outside, across the street, a commuter train rolls off the tracks, down an ivy-covered mound into the street. The ivy starts growing over the train, then grows into the restaurant towards my feet. Trixie continues cutting.

Daphne

The Jeep Cherokee's deflated tires sunk into the sand as the chassis creaked over the uneven dunes. There was a secret stretch of beach that lead to a peninsula, where the party was supposed to be. We had just graduated high school and were taking a week to travel to different beaches so we could really start to drink seriously.

When we saw embers ahead of us, rising above one of the larger dunes into the night sky, we found the closest place to stop where the sand seemed a little more solid. We unpacked the cases of warm beer; the half empty handles of cheap liquor and carried it towards the light. We were greeted by a couple of shadowy-faced, half-clothed boys, who asked for one of my friends, "I don't know who you all are, but if you're Anna's friends, you're cool, come with us, come on over." "Yea, we're with her, her friends, yea, thanks."

A few others were sitting around a poorly made small fire that struggled in the wind. The pit had not been dug deep enough. One of the girls screamed when she saw us, "Anna! This is awesome, you finally made it!" We all introduced ourselves, immediately forgetting everyone's name. A guy told the two of us carrying the booze to put it up near the eroding barrier dune about 20 yards away.

We saw the glass and aluminum flickering with the waves. Then we both noticed there was a slight girl staring out into the ocean, sitting next to everything, with her hand twisting the cap to a handle of vodka on and off. We approached her. "Hey, I don't know either of you." She said, matter-of-factly. My friend answered quickly, "Yea, we're Anna's friends, is this the bar?" "Yea I don't know her... Just leave it in the sand somewhere." She moved her handle out of the way as we dug the bottles and the cardboard box of beer into the sand. She kept staring, this time past us, down the beach. She wore a black dress and had straight black hair and black eye make-up, but somehow she didn't seem to be trying to dress like Robert Smith. "I'm Lisanna, Pat's younger sister." Her brooding eyes looked up. "Oh, cool, good to meet you...see ya down there." We grabbed a couple of beers and walked back to the fire. Although we didn't say it to each other, we were both immediately attracted to this mysterious girl, if only because she seemed at ease with what we saw as anti-social behavior. She seemed dangerous to us. Maybe she was a model. Maybe she was shy.

We got back to the group and everyone got to drinking. We turned the music up loud, tried to flirt with the blonde girls we had forgotten the names of, and talked about our summer jobs, where we were headed in the fall. At one point we reenacted our prom photos. Guys wrapped their arms around the waists of the girls, then guys with guys, girls with girls. Eventually, we started running towards the darkness of the crashing waves. One person would run towards the wake, jump, and stop at the last moment. Then some other guy would pick up a girl or one of his smaller male friends and carry them to the edge and drop them right where the waves broke. Even Lisanna found this amusing, grinning slightly as she stood to the side with the water up to her knees, holding up her long black dress.

It got late and the group's energy started to fade. We all sat around the fire telling embarrassing stories about our friends to the others we didn't know. I looked across the dying fire and saw Lisanna, her eyes barely open, trying to smile and follow the conversation. I nudged my friend who was still talking to one of the blonde girls. "What? She's drunk, I'm drunk, and you should be drunker." He turned back continuing to whisper to his new friend. I waited a moment, then stood up and screamed, "Let's dance!" and turned on that song from Footloose. Everyone laughed and got up and danced, kicking up sand. And I saw her jump up, but then fall back onto her towel. I went over to take her hand, but she was on her back, smiling with her eyes closed, wriggling to the music. "Let's get you up." And as I tried pulling her up, she whispered, "Get Pat." And she went limp and fell back into the sand.

The music was still blaring and everyone was dancing. I ran up to the guy that I thought was Pat. "Hey your sister's not doing well. She passed out." "Where, Let me see." I pointed as we walked back to her. "Hey, sis, shit, you drank too much, you dumbass." We wrapped her in the beach towels carried her over to the barrier dune. "Make her drink some water from my water bottle. I'll be right back." I tried talking to her. She was unresponsive. Her long, shiny black hair had gotten a lot of sand and even some sea grass in it. It seemed like a long time before Pat came back with his keys. "This was her first time drinking, I think." He casually added, as he picked her up and scrambled over the dune to his car. The headlights bounced as they drove off into the night. I looked back and everyone was still fooling around near the shore, and no one had really noticed any of what had happened.

I walked back down to them in disbelief. "Hey where'd your girlfriend go?" My friend asked me, patting my shoulder. "No, she's...uh...drank too much." Anna quickly looked concerned. "Is she alright? We should have looked out for her, that poor girl." "I'm not sure...I think so..."

The night had ended. We all packed up, buried the fire and one of us drove back to Anna's parents' house, drunk. One couple stayed out on the beach. We all learned a couple days later it was alcohol poisoning. She had almost died. None of us saw her again, but I heard she works for a French fashion magazine.

Young Narcissus

My family drove halfway across the country.
Our last stop was always Connecticut.
My mother's friend had a modern house
with a pool, deep in a lush suburban forest.
The trees were glazed in the late August
humidity, even the water looked fetid.
I always jumped in and swam as fast as I could
to the other side, as my parents drank
languidly under the yellow patio umbrella.
But, I wasn't Cheever's Swimmer, I just stopped.
I was too young and not restless enough,
still wondering how pond skaters never sank.

Neighborhood

I'm in the backseat of a black SUV with my parents, as my elderly aunt and uncle drive us through a wealthy suburban neighborhood we might want to move to. As we turn a corner and go down a steep hill to a more isolated and heavily forested road, the large, symmetrical colonial homes begin to change from mostly white with modest dark blue or green shutters to pastel pink or yellow with white shutters. The houses begin to look like dollhouses. My aunt parks the car in front of the only home that still has a dusting of snow on the shrubbery and the green patio furniture cushions. We all sit down on the front patio and a bowl of grapes is passed around as everyone takes turns spitting out the seeds. Soon, three young black men wearing grey-hooded sweatshirts walk by on the sidewalk, all swigging fifths of liquor. One yells to us, "What kind of medicine you got?" I respond, "We don't got any." Looking irritated, they all begin to walk onto the lawn, towards us. I wake myself up, worried I'll dream of something I'll regret.

It's After the End of The World

A Found Poem

Jazz By Sun Ra
Visits Planet Earth
Bad and Beautiful

When Sun Comes Out
Horizon
Monorails and Satellites

We Travel the Space Ways
Interstellar Low Ways
The Other Planes of There

Nothing Is
Somewhere Else
Strange Celestial Road

Strange Strings
When Angels Speak of Love
Cosmic Tones for Mental Therapy

Fate in a Pleasant Mood
Holiday for Soul Dance
Some Blues But Not the Kind That's Blue

Purple Night
Blue Delight
Black Myth/Out in Space

Black Harold and the White Chalk

After Crockett Johnson's Harold and the Purple Crayon

All this black
kid lacks
is a piece of chalk.

A way to talk
about what will be
his boundaries—

a single line
that breaks the spine
of the dark.

His own spark,
in a black world
of lessening doom—

Draw the moon,
draw a home,
draw a bed.

Choose to sleep.
Have a picnic
that won't make you sick.

Frame the city
in your pretty
vision. Don't let

the cop mis-direct
you. Choose your path,
drop the chalk,

and rest.

The House in the Middle (1954)

After a short film produced by the Civil Defense Authority

The tidier house withstands a nuclear blast.

We lived.

Spiritual Structuralism

"Form and function should be one."
—Frank Lloyd Wright

I.

A man painted himself
into an empty room.

So the room was not empty.

It had a bed, a nightstand,
a chair, a rug, and then the man.

The man did not want to create
a space, he wanted to create himself

in a space. And the man called
himself an artist. And he was

an artist, not an architect.

II.

Man is animal from the waist down.
Humanity from the waist up.

My philosophy is sound,
but we're all insecure.

Out of the ground and into
the light, learning to see into, not at.

To see apostles of ourselves
in nature is to be Usonian.

My philosophy is sound,
but let's make some parallels.

White People on "Race"

I am walking in Midtown Manhattan with a childhood friend that I don't see very often. We catch up on how our folks are, how our siblings are doing in other parts of the country. We are walking towards a Cambodian sandwich shop for lunch. Then, my friend asks me if I remember this guy with whom we used to wait at the bus stop, back when we were kids. I say no, not really. Then, a couple minutes later we greet him in front of the shop, "Hey, man, long time no see, doing well, good, good. This place good? Good, good." My friend goes to the restroom and we get in line and try to fill in some of the gaps from the past 15 years. "Where'd you go to College? O yea? Where you work now? Healthcare, cool, cool." I notice a small TV playing sports highlights above the counter. Serena Williams has just lost a match, in a shocking upset. There's a lull in the conversation. I say, "What an upset, huh?" He responds with the same nonchalance, "What a gorilla, woo." I give an uncomfortable chuckle, thinking that he might be being brazenly ironic, "Yea, I'm not sure black women prefer to be called that…" He goes on, "I mean look at those arms and that grunting…" As I am still processing my shock, someone calls out our number for our order. My friend comes back and asks us if we remember a teacher from our grade school. And nothing more comes of the exchange. They start talking about golf and after lunch we all part ways.

A Painting I Can't Get Out of My Head

After Ernie Barnes

There is a slender black woman in an apricot negligee
showing off her elongated stroll on a city park's trail in twilight.
There is a warm breeze that rustles the summer elm trees,
which blows back her white pilot's scarf. She smiles, eyes
closed in daydream, on a hill overlooking her ashen, rust belt city.

Tuesday Morning

After Richard Brautigan

I'm trying to shave
but my face
is pressed
up against
the mirror.

In the kitchen
there is a pumpkin
in a clean
empty, white
refrigerator.

The pumpkin
does not rot.

The Wealthy Alumnus

I am walking around the Pennsylvania campus of my alma mater when a passing student hands me a flyer. It lists the names of my classmates in order of highest to lowest salaries, and also notes the exact address where each one of us lives. The first fifteen alums are highlighted, and at the top of the flyer it suggests visiting any of them, at anytime, so you can "see how well they're doing". The highest earner lives about an hour north, so I drive up to find a large white colonial house on the side of a hill with an apple orchard surrounding the property. There are yard signs lining the drive: "#1 Earner of the Class of 2011". I wait in the empty driveway for fifteen minutes as the sun sets. Then I hear a revving engine coming up the hill. A little red sports car stops at the nearby intersection, and I think the driver and I make brief eye contact, but it's difficult to tell because of the glare and his sunglasses. I nod slightly and the light turns green and he steps on the gas, but instead of turning right into the driveway, the car goes straight, off the road, through a chicken wire fence and into a thick telephone pole. I hear the horrible crushing of metal and the shattering of the windshield, and I see his body shoot forward through the glass in slow motion, as he lies on the hood of the steaming, wrecked car, covered in blood. I run inside to call 911, and there is a group of smiling alums, all with name tags, and as I'm about to tell them what I saw, they throw their hands up and say, "Oh great, you finally made it!"

Nursery Rhyme

3 little

    monkeys

        jumping

on the bed
1

     fell off
     and got

        a tracheotomy

     another 1

         a vasectomy

     and another

         a lobotomy

THE DIFFERENCE BETWEEN A CHURCH AND A HOSPITAL

             some pot-

          bellied skele-
tons.

        Chum with me

on the shoulders
   of our fathers

WAVES COAST THE LIGHT

cannibals finally

                            check out chicken

                as fingers shake,
                "End with the tonic."

the center   of the universe   smells of raspberries

                                    tastes like rum.

Failing Institutions

The son of a son of failed senator steers
his '27 Chris-Craft classic, bubbling over blue,

making his way back, under the pink backlit
suspension bridge, almost chewable,
swaying in the foggy harbor breeze.

It is a record cruel day in June
in a nation with no patience.

The mallet-fisted, billy-clubbing Irish cop
tickets each ugly duckling for jaywalking.

And the shoulder-squeezing Italian politician,
with the tic-tac-toe tie, never admits defeat.

There's a formality in the flesh
of comets, when they careen into the marketplace.

The premium redemption? CASH—
For your bottles and cans.

The bum cries by the nickel, dies by the dime,
singing his own country song,

"Scrambled eggs and whiskey
is what I'll have for breakfast, now that she's gone.
She never let me in, on her own propensity..."

And then the son dives in for a buttered watermelon.
The sea-soaked loam imbeds into his Nantucket Reds.

But, if this is truly a madras-ed matter,
we'll leave it for the tennis courts to decide.
Above the chaos of this continual execution room

there is a glazed-over, tryptophan-look to Orion,
as he loosens his hunting belt another notch,
expanding the universe, just a little more.

Written in Blue Ink on a Day During Trump's Presidential Bid

I'm starting to think
words are, in fact,
the ocean, the plain-
colored spaces between,

the land.

I'm starting
a new

c   o   u   n   t   r   y

The Poetry of America

Salvador Dalí, 1943

America loves African blood. A massacre of innocents
with peanuts like bits of shelled data in a cruncher's stadium.

Black cosmic athletes breastfeed on the spillage of Coca-Cola
while trying not to call out to the crotches that can't be ignored.

Dame un agujero, un cuarto, un tocador, why is my back so sore!
What kind of nerves can be found when we open the sciatic drawer?

The stuffed patriotic skeleton dances wick-headed and puppet-legged
in a tight uniform of taut skin under a green-eyed megalithic melting.

And in the desert, Adonis contemplates his pole, or is it a javelin?
All eggs can soar, gently, but it was the wild boar that killed him.

More White People on "Race"

I move across the country and I'm invited to dinner at a family friend's house. I've only met this woman a few times in my life, but she promises a good meal and some advice about living in the area. When I show up to her home, she greets me with a big hug and welcomes me into the living room, where her elderly father is sitting, smiling politely and another woman, who I've never met before, but is introduced as "another friend that I'll have to introduce to your mother." This woman greets me, sips wine and then looks pleasantly out the window. They all ask me about my new job and tell me that I'll love living here, all of the natural beauty. We sit down for dinner, and I comment on how I love how fresh the vegetables are around here. I offhandedly add, "Those pickers, they really do some hard work." That is when the family friend responds, "Yea, they do. This salad should be great." Then something comes to her mind and she continues, "But you know, we need to live in a meritocracy. We now live in an age where I can't fire a black guy if he's doing a bad job because then I'm a racist. But, yeah I know Mexicans work really hard, still are poor. Who commits the crimes? A lot of Blacks, some Mexicans. Let me tell you a quick story. I was flying across the country to close up my summer home for the season and take my car off the island. It was a nightmare. Sitting on the tarmac because some people's luggage was put on the wrong plane. And we're sitting there and I see out of the window this guy just shuffling, whistling along, bringing over a couple of bags. Stop dawdling, José! I paid money, move your ass! I know most of them work hard. Pedro on my lawn. Frieda and her sister do the house. But we just need a list of them who are lazy, living off my taxes. Kick them out. Every Welfare González, Lazy Santiago, Moochin' Muñoz,...", "Stealin' Sanchez", I add. "No, no you don't count. You're not like that." There is a moment of silence as she begins to clear the plates. I begin to help. "Sit down, I got it. I got it." She says. "Would anyone like any dessert, coffee?" And we all say yes, and try to smile politely.

The Overturned Red Wheelbarrow

Chickens, white, beside water
Rain glazed barrow wheel
Red, upon so much depends

Like Living In Someone Else's House or They Used to Own, Now You Rent

You pay the rent, but he says he gave you a discount.
He gave you the master bedroom with a walk-in closet
but it's because he can't walk up the flight of stairs anymore.

In the morning you tiptoe to the shared kitchen
to make your coffee, and while at the faucet, you remember,
he said that the water is undrinkable, "It's too hard."

He sleeps downstairs, where he can hear the floorboards creak.
He has a cleaning lady come every week,
but she skips your room because you leave your books on the bed.

After work, you come home and make dinner.
Weeks pass, then he asks you not to use, "the good plates."
He adds that, "they're only for company."

You do laundry on the weekends and he leaves his soiled clothes
in the washer, and when he asks you to wash his with yours,
he adds, "Sort it out for me, would you?"

Retired Meatpacking Magnate in Mexico, 1925

"I don't suppose I shall ever be happy. Perhaps no one ever is. The thing that would make me happiest just now would be to know that I could get roaring drunk and wander about the Loop for two days without anyone paying attention to me."
—J. Ogden Armour

Pluvial days and snakebite nights
Leaves blown through a cocoa dusk
(Here's an excerpt of it all—*whoosh!*)

and a howler charged over to pound
his chest in wild vibrato growl, like a well-
greased timpani in the back of a half-shell.

My newspaper winged itself out-
of-here and this century's speeding
like red horses down the beach.

Get away from my window! Now!
There are watercolor stains on the lip
of my coffee cup, each drip, irrationally

exuberant. I don't know what to do
with you with your clothes all on!
Are there any stray packs of dogs?

An Irish wolfhound dug up the jaw
of a remembered poet and so I will
roll my "r's" in liberation and not punch

at the tarantulas as big as typewriters
and so even the deaf will know
that banana-leaf crackle of a phonograph.

Telegraphic Brevity

A Found Poem

J. Austin Sullivan
of Altoona, Pa.,

a student
at Dickinson College

was brutally beaten

by ten negroes
last night. His skull

is frac-
tured

and he is other-
wise injured.

It is fear-
ed he will not

recover.

—*New York Times*, March 22nd 1897

Hand Crutches at a Little League Game

My father walks down from the metal bleachers to the umpire, "Do you fully understand the implications of the call you just made?" As this is happening, a sky blue Pontiac drives to short centerfield. The door swings open and hand crutches, one by one, are thrown out. Then an old babysitter, with a white-haired permanent, smoking a cigarette, balances on the edge of the car's door frame, making a diving motion as the car sways. She jumps out and the trunk pops open. She walks around and pulls out two more hand crutches that she throws towards the pitcher's mound. I'm still standing in the batter's box, waiting for another pitch, but all the other players have disappeared.

WRITTEN IN CAPITALS SO YOU'LL UNDERSTAND

For Christian Bok

FLUXUS FUCKED US FUCKED YOU UP UBU'S FUCKED UP TOO

GUTTURAL UTTERANCES UDDER-WINCES ANOTHER GUTTERAIL
SUBSTANCELESS

MONGREL MONGOLOID MONDALE DEVOID AVOIDING SONG
ALTOGETHER

SNAIL MAIL MEANING MASCULINE MESCALINE A MASS CULLING
MASSIVE DIN

BOK BOK BOK BOK BOK STOP!

YOU SCARED? WHY'D YOU STOP MAKING SENSE?

CONFINED AND FINED YOURSELF YOU COULDN'T FIND YOURSELF
COULDN'T

FIND ANOTHER METHOD OF SELF-EXPRESSION

"Who Else has Memories of Pistol-Whipping Hunters?"

For P.W.

As your single dad mixed brownie batter for us, you said,
there were roosters loose in your bedroom, you said,
"As a communist, I'll learn to live in a Grandfather clock."

Wide-eyed, you continued, "Landslides will wreck the carpet
and every time you sneeze in the winter, you'll split your lip. Shhh…
equal and opposite forces are at work, I'm being followed."

And I remember that ongoing white noise of your living room,
Turner Classic Movies was on in fuzzy black and white
and no one was ever watching, but no one could turn it off.

Milk, Blood, Water

I.

A milk truck runs over a ghost
in front of my old house.

Or is it a man
with a sheet over his head?

White struck white
and white flowed out.

And is that blood?
It's a coagulating thought.

II.

It is a black man.
His skin and the street

have met yet again.
There is a pallid color

to all dead men.
There is also the blood,

that seeps down the road,
into the water at its' source.

III.

Strings are laid down
over the neck of a river.

I strum in the current,
a music of understanding.

I'm getting wet!
But I am not an egoist.

I am myself, becoming
aware of the waters.

A Bigger Splash

David Hockney, 1967

Where did this memory come from?
Did it effervesce and spurt up, a semi-
recollection displaced by a diver?
Or is this memory the diver himself,
plunging, away from the yellow springboard?

I don't believe in the force of this torque,
or that I'll ever watch from that director's chair.
I won't even walk through the sliding glass
doors into the cool of a pink house and look out
to contemplate the California dust.

I still am only remembering this image, apart
from its' context. A disturbance disappearing.

The shadows of this splash do not make a movie,
no one is there, you are the one in the water.

Suburban Sutra

Do the train suicides of affluenza dive onto the tracks?
Tell me not the secret that I ask.

Could these future fisher kings not cope with a stocked lake?
Tell me not the secret that I ask.

What were the boys' last dreams, as they took off?
Tell me not the secret that I ask.

I have felt like the boy with the toy hand grenade,
feeling awkward in the overalls that hang off my body.

I have been just a stick figure self in a blooming park,
lightly sketched with clenched fists and tired veins.

—

Were lilacs truly Walt's favorite? Allen's, sunflowers?
Tell me not the secret that I ask.

That innocent beauty of proto-homosexuality
grabbing each other in your parent's master bedroom!

O the secret and the profane!
Tell me not the secret that I ask.

—

In the Twilight Zone episode, *Eye of the Beholder,*
we awake, head bandaged, then uncovered, blurry-eyed,

we see pig-faced people shudder at our ugliness,
then there is a shot that pans out the window

to the Brutalist architecture of a planned utopian society.
Just because you're asleep isn't proof of the night.

So when I wander through the cold of my hometown,
where the old jewelry stores have turned into banks,

and the luxury car dealerships have turned into banks,
I remember I was born into a gulag of opulence.

See there are no 'sides' to the tracks, yet no shipments out.
Just another raw, painful April at dusk.

—

As I walk Market Square, I wonder if I grew up
in a sundown town. (This remains unclear.)

Recently, a member of the town council scoffed
at the black woman hired as high school principal,

saying she was "a self-described descendent of slaves."
Just because you're asleep, isn't proof of the night.

Another council member, a realtor, in blinding Lily Pulitzer
and pearls said she encouraged a young black couple to move up

to town, to a pink Adler estate with a lily-padded koi pond
and a spitting devil's head fountain encircled by pink gravel.

"Why wouldn't they move in? The summers are spectacular."
Tell me not the secret that I ask.

—

There was a sense that breaking and entering was wrong,
but those backyard gardens with those 10 ft. manicured shrubs

were tall enough to sneak around in the humid moonlight;
the shelves of long pools extending from the Georgian portico

down to the lake made it seem the pristine was untouchable,
and we were supposed to be enacting our own riotousness

to look back on. Wrestling with ourselves naked, with just
the leaves in our hair and stuck to our sweaty, grimy chests,

somehow instinctively we knew, Anne Carson's maxim,
"To live past the end of your own myth is a perilous thing."

—

Fatal Attraction is really an allegory for the deep malaise
brought on by a move to the posh suburbs.

The quick urges of the city overwhelm you enough to boil
a small pet, make you stay at the office past your last train home.

Finally, the city puts on a white dress, gets shot into a bathtub.
Tell me not the secret that I ask.

—

There is a definite hard soil season that moves into spring.
In the bleak corn stubble, just outside town, thin ice

covers footsteps. Frogs have stopped their hearts in the heel.
Our pale cheeks tighten, our chins become more prominent.

"Ah! sunflower weary of time…Where the youth pined
away with desire, …arise from the graves and aspire."

—

I walk past my old stucco home, it's for sale again,
a lawn care truck with the same last name as mine

is parked in front, as the crew works on the hydrangeas.
Tell me not the secret that I ask.

I remember my Grandmother coming up for Christmas.
We'd decorate sugar cookies with BB-like silver sprinkles.

When they cooled, we'd grab a couple. Grandma'd call
my sister, "fatty", puff up her cheeks like a squirrel.

Later we'd be watching basketball and she'd ask,
"Why are all the players black?" and my Mom would follow,

"Who came up with these names? Davarius, LaDainian, Deonte?"
Tell me not the secret that I ask.

—

Meanwhile, in a basement with a walk-in wine cooler, across town,
after a classical piano lesson, a young girl plays her first jazz chord.

Why was it that when I heard on my bedroom boombox
the trumpet trill of Miles Davis' *Will o' the Wisp*

I simultaneously felt more Spanish, more American, more human?
Tell me not the secret that I ask.

—

So commuter train teenage suicides of affluenza,
Giacometti once said, "The legs are only the mind's

antennae to the earth." You all jumped, I guess
oppressive impotence by the lake; was this just your last cast out?

Did you, too, hear faint hissing of these languorous lawns?
Tell me not the secret that I ask. I have a train to catch.

First Poem

The first poem I remember writing
was entitled, "I See America Healing."
It was in the week or so after 9/11
and my 7th grade English teacher
was half-assing it through the poetry unit.

She force-fed us our Langston, our Emily,
some Frost, maybe an Angelou, or two,
but Whitman went down smooth.
"The varied carols I hear, those of the firemen
putting out fires, so brave, …/The policemen…"

It didn't make much sense,
to begin a consciousness with healing,
to change a democratic chant into elegy,
but, if anything, poetry calls for reconsideration.

Notes:

In "After RIOT", Dr. Chala Holland is the Principal of Lake Forest High School.

In the found poem, "The Legend of the Happy Swimming Pool", the entire poem is alineated transcript of James Dickey's side of a conversation between him and Robert Lowell. On YouTube it is entitled, "James Dickey and Robert Lowell Discuss Dreams, c. 1969.", but it is a clip from the documentary film by Stan Croner called, "Lord, Let Me Die But Not Die Out".

In "Lake Forest Chainsaw Massacre", the quotations are taken from *Chicago Tribune, New York Times,* and *People Magazine* articles from May/June 1987.

In "Structural Spiritualism", some of the language is taken from Frank Lloyd Wright in an interview from June 1957.

In the found poem, "It's After the End of the World", each line, including the title, is a title of a Sun Ra album.

In "Who Else has Memories of Pistol-whipping Hunters?", P.W. was a childhood friend who showed early signs of paranoid schizophrenia. The title was taken from a Facebook post.

In the found poem, "Telegraphic Brevity", J. Austin Sullivan is my Great Grandfather and my namesake.

In "Retired Meatpacking Magnate in Mexico, 1925", J. Ogden Armour had the second largest family fortune in the world in 1919. By 1921, he had lost most of it, at one point, losing a million dollars a day for 130 days.

In "Suburban Sutras", the refrain, "Tell me not the secret that I ask" is taken from the last line of the poem, "The Mystery" by Paul Laurence Dunbar.

Austin Sanchez-Moran was born in Washington, D.C., and raised in Lake Forest, Il. He is a product of an East Coast boarding school, and then went on to receive a BA in Philosophy from Gettysburg College and an MFA in Creative Writing from George Mason University. He was a Lannan Fellow and Honors Fellow at GMU. He has taught English in many places around the world, including Granada, Spain; Guangzhou, China; California and Utah. Most recently, he has taught at Hebron Academy in rural Western Maine and is now teaching at Choate Rosemary Hall in suburban Wallingford, Connecticut. Suburban Sutras is his first collection of poetry.

His poetry and short fiction has appeared in: *45th Parallel Journal, Best Micro Fiction 2020, Best New Poets of the Midwest 2017, Catamaran Literary Review, Denver Quarterly, Ekphrastic Review, Fjords Review, The Laurel Review, Linden Avenue Literary Journal, Maudlin House, Midwestern Gothic, Rawboned, RHINO Poetry 2018, Rivet Journal, Salamander Magazine, Soledad Inmates' Journal, Sundial Review, The Texas Review, Wild Age Press, Yalobusha Review,* and *Yemassee Journal.* He is thankful to all of these publications for acknowledging his work.

www.ingramcontent.com/pod-product-compliance
Lightning Source LLC
Chambersburg PA
CBHW021159090426
42740CB00008B/1160